THE LITTLE
BLACK BOOK OF

DOG
JOKES

A Compendium of Waggish Wit
& Shaggy Stories

WRITTEN AND COMPILED BY
SUZANNE SCHWALB

ILLUSTRATED BY
ELAINE LOPEZ

 PETER PAUPER PRESS, INC.
WHITE PLAINS, NEW YORK

For my canine comedians
Clarence and Eli

Thanks to Barbara, Lois, Marc, & Vicki
for the contributions

Designed by Heather Zschock

Copyright © 2009
Peter Pauper Press, Inc.
202 Mamaroneck Avenue
White Plains, NY 10601
All rights reserved
ISBN 978-1-59359-838-9
Printed in Hong Kong
7 6 5 4 3 2 1

Visit us at www.peterpauper.com

THE LITTLE BLACK BOOK OF

DOG JOKES

Contents

introduction

ark, bark. Woof, woof. Sniff, sniff. Wag, wag. Besides being man's best friends, our canine companions turn out to be some of the world's best comedians, from puppy antics that convulse us into giggles, to the pranks of older furry friends that keep us chortling at life's follies. Here is a book to celebrate them all. *The Little Black Book of Dog Jokes* is a compact treasury of canine humor that simply takes the biscuit. Packed with dog jokes, dog riddles, quips, quotes, "dogma," and doggerel, it's guaranteed to have you howling with laughter. So— let the heeling begin! Happy tails!

speak!

JOKES ABOUT TALKING DOGS

A guy was about to go into a bar when a dog tugged at his pants leg and said, "Hey, pal! Wanna make some easy money?"

The man couldn't believe it. "You can *talk?*" he asked the dog.

"Yeah," the dog answered, "and that's how we're gonna pick up some quick cash. Just take me into the bar with you, pretend I'm your dog, and bet everybody in the place that I can talk."

"Great idea!" said the man. He took the canine into the bar with him, set it on a table, and announced to everyone that his dog could talk. Of course, the other patrons didn't believe him, and it wasn't long before several thousand dollars had been wagered.

Finally, after all bets had been placed, the guy said to the dog, "All right. Go ahead—say something."

The dog looked at him but wouldn't say a word.

"Hey!" said the guy. "The bets are placed. Say something, for crying out loud!"

The dog looked at him and said nothing.

Disgusted, the guy paid all the bets, scooped up the dog, and left the bar. Once outside, he yelled at the animal, "You just cost me over a thousand dollars! What have you got to say for yourself?"

"Take it easy, pal! You ain't thinkin'," replied the dog. "Tomorrow night, we'll get odds of five to one or better."

A man is walking down the street when he hears a voice: "Pssst, come over here!"

He looks around but sees no one, just an old greyhound.

"Yeah! Over here!" says the greyhound. "Look at me tied up here. I should be racing. I won twenty races in my career, you know?"

The man thinks to himself, "Holy cow, a talking dog. I have to have it; it will make me rich!" So he finds the owner and says, "I'd like to buy your dog. Is he for sale?"

The owner says, "No, friend, you don't want that old thing!"

"But I do!" insists the man. "I'll give you a thousand dollars for him."

"OK," sighs the owner, "but I think you're making a big mistake."

Handing over the money, the man says, "Why do you think that?"

Says the owner, "Because that dog's a damn liar. It never won a race in its life!"

A man and his dog walk into a bar. The man proclaims to the bartender, "I'll bet you a round of drinks my dog can talk." The bartender says, "Sure! Go ahead." The man asks the dog, "What covers a house?"

The dog answers, "Roof!"

The man asks the dog, "How does sandpaper feel?"

The dog answers, "Rough!"

The man asks the dog, "Who was the greatest ball player of all time?"

The dog answers, "Ruth!"

"There you go," says the man to the bartender, "pay up. I told you he could talk." The annoyed barkeep throws them both out.

Out on the sidewalk, the dog looks at the man and asks, "Or was it DiMaggio?"

A man went into a bar in which there were only a dog, a cat, and the bartender.

As the man placed his order, the dog lapped up the remains of a beer, stifled a yawn, said, "So long, Jack," and strolled out.

The man was stunned. "Did you hear that?" he said to the bartender. "That dog talked!"

"Don't be a fool," said the bartender. "Dogs can't talk."

"I *heard* him," the man protested.

"You just *think* you heard him," insisted the barkeep. "It's really that smart alec cat over there. He's a ventriloquist."

A Jack Russell went to the employment agency to look for work.

"I need a job," he said to the man behind the desk.

The man's jaw dropped. "A talking dog!" he said. "I'll fix you up with something in no time."

After several minutes on the phone, the man announced, "You're all set! You start at the circus on Monday."

"That's no good," protested the Jack Russell. "I'm a plumber."

A new dog owner couldn't wait to show off his pet to his friend. When the friend finally came over, the man called the dog. The pup burst into the room and sat before his new master, tail wagging.

The man pointed to a pair of slippers by the couch and ordered, "Fetch!"

At once the tail stopped wagging. The dog hung his head. He looked up disapprovingly at his master. "*Oy!*" the pup whined. "My tail hurts from wagging it so much. And that gourmet dog food you're giving me is absolutely tasteless. And you haven't taken me for a good long walk in at least a week. . . ."

The friend was astounded. "Your dog talks!" he said.

"Yes, but he's young and I'm still training him," explained the man. "He thought I said 'Kvetch!'"

Two dogs were talking during break time at obedience school. "The thing I hate about obedience school," one said to the other, "is that you learn all this stuff you'll never use in the real world."

dog riddles

Q: What has four legs and one arm?

A: A happy pit bull.

Q: What do you get when you cross a pit bull with a collie?

A: A dog that rips your arm off, then goes for help.

Q: Why don't dogs make good dancers?

A: Because they have two left feet.

Q: What do you get when you cross
a rottweiler with a hyena?

A: I don't know, but if it laughs I'll join in.

Q: What's the difference between a
new wife and a new dog?

A: After a year, the dog's still excited to see
you.

Q: What do you get when you cross
a dog with a journalist?

A: A Rover reporting.

Q: Why did the Doberman marry
    the golden retriever?

A: He found her very fetching.

Q: Why did the dog cross the road
    twice?

A: He was trying to fetch a boomerang.

Q: How do you make a puppy dis-
    appear?

A: Use Spot remover.

Q: What does a Dalmatian say after eating a particularly savory bowl of dog food?

A: Oh yeah, that definitely hits the spots.

Q: What's fast, furry, and goes "foow, foow?"

A: A dog chasing a car that's in reverse.

Q: What's the difference between a businessman and a warm dog?

A: The businessman wears a suit, the dog just pants.

Q: What did Dorothy do when her dog got stuck?

A: She called a Toto truck.

Q: What happened when the dog went to the flea circus?

A: He stole the show!

DOG DAZE
As Seen on Real-Life
Dog License Applications

Alaskan Malibu

Bagel

Basket Hound

Belgian Malenoise

Black Labrador *(dog was a yellow Lab)*

Borderline Collie

Carrion Terrier *(instead of cairn terrier)*

Chevy King Charles *(instead of
    Cavalier King Charles)*

Copper Spaniel

Dorky Terrier

El Paso *(meant Lhasa Apso)*

German Police Man

Great Pekinese *(supposed to be Pyrenees)*

Great Pyramid

Highland Heeler

Irish Settler

Jack Daniels Terrier

Lopso Apso

Miniature Datsun

Palmeranian

Rhode Island Ridgeback *(instead of
    Rhodesian Ridgeback)*

Rockwelders

Rottenwiler

****-Sue

Welch Corgi

Westminster Terrier

Wild-Haired Terrier

Wineamimer

every dog has its day

A man walked into a bar one day and asked, "Does anyone here own the Rottweiler outside?"

"Yeah!" snarled a biker, standing up. "I do! What about it?"

"I think my Chihuahua just killed him," says the first man.

"Whaddaya mean?" the biker spat. "How could your little runt kill my Rottweiler?"

"Well, it seems he got stuck in your dog's throat!"

A little man walked into a bar with his pet under his arm. "Look at that silly dog," sneered a burly guy with a pit bull. "Look at that long nose and those stumpy legs. That's the ugliest dog I've ever seen."

"Yeah?" said the little man bravely. "I'll have you know he's real mean."

"Don't make me laugh!" said the burly man. "I'll bet you fifty dollars my pit bull can finish him off in two minutes."

"OK. You're on."

The stumpy-legged dog and the pit bull lined up nose to nose. Suddenly, the shorter animal lunged forward and bit the pit bull in half. The owner couldn't believe it. "What kind of dog is that anyway?" he growled.

"Well, before I cut off his tail, he was an alligator."

Q: How many dogs does it take to change a light bulb?

A: Rottweiler: Go ahead. Make me.

Golden retriever: The day is young, the sun is shining, we've got our whole lives ahead of us . . . and you're worrying about a burned-out light bulb?

Border collie: Just one. Me. And I'll re-wire anything not up to code.

Lab: Oh, let me! Me! Me! Me! Can I? Can I? Huh? Huh? Can I?

Dachshund: I can't reach the damn lamp!

Shih Tzu: Puh-leeze! Let the servants do it, Darling.

Toy poodle: I'll blow in the border collie's ear and he'll do it. By the time he finishes re-wiring everything, my nails will be dry.

Malamute: Let the border collie do it. While he's busy, you can feed me.

Australian shepherd: Get all the light bulbs in a circle . . .

Irish wolfhound: Somebody else do it. I've got a hangover.

Greyhound: It's not moving. Who cares?

Mastiff: Mastiffs are NOT afraid of the dark.

Hound dog: ZZZZZZZZZZZZZ

Old English sheep dog: Light bulb? Light bulb? The thing I just ate was a light bulb?

BARKING UP THE WRONG TREE
Canine Breeds that Didn't Quite Make It

- Collie + Lhasa Apso = Collapso, a fold-up dog you can take anywhere

- Bloodhound + Labrador = Blabador, a dog that won't stop barking

- Pointer + Setter = Poinsetter, a Christmas favorite

- Terrier + Bulldog = Terribull, a breed that's bad to the bone

- Malamute + Pointer = Moot Point, a doubtful sort of breed

- Pekinese + Lhasa Apso = Peekasso, a Cubist dog

- Bull Terrier + Shih Tzu = Bull-shitz, an untrustworthy dog

clever canines

JOKES ABOUT SMART DOGS

A man went into a bar which was empty except for the bartender and a dog playing chess. The man observed the dog eyeing the board with concentration, moving his pieces in his teeth. When he made a good move, he wagged his tail with excitement, and when a "Check!" was called for, he gave a brisk bark.

Flabbergasted, the man exclaimed, "Hey, that's a smart dog you've got there!"

The bartender answered, "He's not that smart! I've beat him three times out of five so far."

A man went into a bar and noticed three men and a dog playing cards. The dog was playing exceptionally well. "That is one smart dog," the man remarked.

"He's not that smart," replied one of the players. "Every time he gets a good hand, he wags his tail."

Four dog-owners were discussing how intelligent their pets were. The first, an accountant, said his dog, "Calculator," was smart. The bean counter told the canine to fetch a dozen dog biscuits, bring them back, and divide them into piles of three, which the dog did with no problem.

The second dog owner, a chemist, agreed that the first dog was smart, but insisted her pooch, "Test Tube," was, too. She then commanded it to fetch a quart of milk and pour six ounces into a ten-ounce glass. The dog did this easily.

The third professional, an engineer, said her dog was just as smart. At her command, the dog, named "Blueprint," retrieved paper and pen and drew up the plans for an A-frame dog chalet.

All three agreed that their dogs were equally smart. Then they turned to the fourth dog owner, a union member, and asked, "What can your dog do?"

The teamster called his dog, named "Break Time," and said, "Show 'em your stuff." Break Time ate the biscuits, drank the milk, relieved himself on the paper, claimed he injured his back, filed a grievance for unsafe working conditions, applied for Worker's Comp, and went home on sick leave.

A local business looking for help put a sign in the window that said: "HELP WANTED. Must be able to type, be good with a computer, and be bilingual. We are an Equal Opportunity Employer."

A short time later, a dog trotted up to the window, looked at the sign, and went inside. He sat before the receptionist, wagged his tail, walked back to the sign, and whined. Getting the idea, the receptionist called for the personnel director. The director was surprised, to say the least, at the sight of the animal, but led him back to his office, where the dog jumped into a chair and sat attentively. "I appreciate your interest in the position," said the director, "but I'm afraid we can't hire you. The sign says you have to type." At this the dog jumped down, went to the typewriter, and proceeded to keystroke a perfect letter. He pulled out the page, trotted over to the director, laid it in his lap, and jumped back in the chair.

The director was stunned, but said, "The sign also says you have to be good with a computer." The dog jumped down again and went to the computer, where it proceeded to demonstrate its expertise with various programs, producing a spreadsheet, database, and slideshow.

By this time the director was dumbfounded. He said to the dog, "I realize you are a very intelligent dog and have some extraordinary abilities. However, I still cannot give you the job."

The dog jumped down, went to a copy of the sign, and put his paw on the sentence that said "Equal Opportunity Employer." The manager said, "Yes, but the sign also says you have to be bilingual."

The dog looked him straight in the eye and said, "Meow."

A butcher sees a dog in his shop and notices that he has a note in his mouth. He takes the note and reads it. It says, "Please give me a dozen sausages and a pound of beef. The money is clipped to this note." The butcher looks, and lo and behold, there is a ten dollar bill clipped to the note. So he takes the money, puts the meat in a bag, and places it in the dog's mouth. The dog leaves, and the butcher, impressed by the animal, decides to close up shop and follow the canine.

He trails the dog down the street until it comes to a crosswalk. The dog jumps up, presses the button, and waits patiently, bag in mouth, for the light to change. It does, and he walks across the street with the butcher behind him.

The dog comes to a bus stop, studies the schedule, then jumps up onto the bus

stop bench to wait. Along comes a bus. The dog gets up, then looks at the bus number, and sits back down. Another bus comes. The dog looks at the number, decides it's the right bus, and climbs into it. The amazed butcher does likewise.

The bus travels through town into the suburbs. The dog watches the scenery. After a while he moves to the front of the bus, stands on his two back paws, and pushes the button to stop the bus. Then he gets off, groceries still in his mouth. Again the butcher follows, stupefied.

The dog walks down a road, turns at a house, proceeds up the sidewalk, and drops the groceries on the front step. Then he goes back down the walk, starts running, and throws himself—whap!—against the door. He goes back once more, starts running, and throws himself—whap!—against the door again. There's no answer. The dog trots down the walk, jumps up on a wall, goes to a window, bumps his head against it several times, jumps off the wall, and goes back to the door to wait.

A big guy throws the door open and starts cussing at the dog. The butcher runs up. "What are you doing?" he says. "Your dog is a genius. He could be on TV, for crying out loud!"

"Genius, my ass," the guy responds. "This is the second time this week he's forgotten his key."

A family accidentally left their front door open and their retriever bolted out. After calling for the dog in vain, the husband got in the car and went in search of the lost Lab.

He cruised the neighborhood for some time with no luck, then pulled up to a couple out walking and inquired if they'd seen the dog.

"You mean the one following your car?" they asked.

An architect, a doctor, and a lawyer were arguing about who had the smartest dog. They decided to settle the issue by getting their dogs together to learn which could perform the most impressive feat.

"All right, Rover," said the architect.

Rover trotted over to a nearby table and constructed a full-scale model of the Empire State Building with toothpicks.

Pretty impressive, everyone agreed, and the architect gave Rover a cookie.

"Go for it, Spot," said the doc.

Spot lost no time in performing an emergency appendectomy on one of the doctor's patients, who came through in fine shape. Not bad, said the trio, and Spot got a cookie from the doc.

"OK, Fella," said the lawyer.

Fella promptly screwed the other two dogs, took their cookies, and went out to lunch.

A man hated his wife's dog and decided to get rid of it. So he put the dog in the car, drove it miles away, and dropped it off. But the dog was already walking up the driveway when he returned home.

The next day, he dropped the dog twice as far away, but the same thing happened. Day after day, he increased the distance. Still the dog kept returning home before him.

Finally, the man simply drove a few miles from home, but turned left, then right, crossed the bridge, took another left, and another, and so on, until he reached the perfect spot. He dropped the dog there.

Hours later, he called his wife at home. "Jane, is the dog there?" he asked.

"Yes," answered the wife. "Why?"

Frustrated, the man said, "Put that dog on the phone. I'm lost and I need directions."

A farmer wondered how many sheep he had, so he asked his Australian shepherd to count.

"What's the verdict?" the farmer inquired when the dog had completed the task.

"Thirty."

"Are you sure?" asked the farmer. "I thought I only had twenty-eight."

"I know," said the Aussie. "I rounded them up."

A woman at a movie theater found she was sitting a row behind a man who was seated next to a large dog. She was astounded to observe that the dog was watching the movie attentively, "woofing" encouragement to the hero, baring his teeth at the bad guy, and drooling during the scenes in the café. After the film, the woman stopped the man and said, "Excuse me, sir, but I couldn't help noticing that your dog was really into that movie."

"Yes," the man replied, "I found it surprising as well. He hated the book."

A border collie went to a Western Union office, took out a blank form, and wrote "Woof, woof, woof, woof, woof, woof, woof, woof, woof."

The clerk studied the form and said, "There are only nine words here. You could send another 'woof' for the same price."

The collie said, "But that would be silly."

I used to look at (my dog) Smokey and think, 'If you were a little smarter you could tell me what you were thinking,' and he'd look at me like he was saying, 'If you were a little smarter, I wouldn't have to.'

—FRED JUNGCLAUS

facts of life

While walking through the park with his father, a young boy noticed two dogs in the act. "What are they doing, Daddy?" he asked. "They are making puppies, son," replied his father.

Several nights later, the lad awoke from a bad dream and went to his parents' bedroom. When he entered, he exclaimed, "Daddy! Why are you on top of Mommy?" Wanting to be honest but brief, the father said, "Your mother and I are trying to make you a baby brother or sister." The youngster said, "Well, flip over, Momma, I want a puppy!"

Father and son were walking hand in hand when they saw two dogs "doing it" in the middle of the street. The flustered dad told his son that the big brown dog hurt his paw and the little gray dog was helping him across the street.

The boy thought a minute, looked up, and said, "Isn't that just like life? You try to help someone and you get screwed!"

A three-year-old boy went with his dad to see a new litter of puppies. On their return home, he informed his mother, "There were four girl puppies and three boy puppies."

"How did you know?" his mother asked.

"Daddy picked them up and looked underneath," he replied. "I think it's printed on their bottoms."

We've begun to long for the
pitter-patter of little feet—
so we bought a dog.
Well, it's cheaper, and you
get more feet.

—RITA RUDNER

DOGS ARE FROM MARS

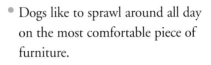

- Dogs like to sprawl around all day on the most comfortable piece of furniture.

- Dogs leave their toys everywhere.

- Dogs can hear a package of food being opened a block away, but they can't hear you when you are in the same room.

- Dogs growl when they are not happy.

- Dogs will love you forever if you rub their tummies.

- Dogs do disgusting things with their mouths and then try to kiss you.

SUMMARY:

Dogs are little men in fur coats.

CATS ARE FROM VENUS

- Cats rarely listen to you.
- Cats are unpredictable.
- When you want to play, cats want to be alone.
- Cats expect you to cater to their every whim.
- Cats leave hair everywhere.
- Cats drive you nuts and cost an arm and a leg.

SUMMARY:

Cats are tiny women in fur coats.

sick puppies

AT THE VET

A lady awoke one morning to find that her dog was not moving. She called her vet, who asked her to bring the animal in. After a brief examination, the vet pronounced the dog dead.

"Are you sure?" asked the agitated woman. "He was a wonderful family pet! Is there nothing else you can do?"

The vet paused. "There is one more thing we can do," he said. He left the room, and then returned, carrying a cage with a cat in it. The vet released the feline, and the cat walked over to the dog, sniffed it from head to toe, and returned to its carrier.

"Well, that confirms it," announced the vet.

"Your dog is dead."

Satisfied the DVM had done everything possible,

the woman sighed and said, "How much do I owe you?"

"That will be $330," said the vet.

"What?!" screamed the woman. "What did you do that cost $330?"

"Well," the vet replied, "it's $30 for the office visit and $300 for the cat scan."

A man takes his Great Dane to the vet and says, "My dog is cross-eyed. Is there anything you can do for him?"

The vet says, "Well, let's have a look." He picked the dog up and examined his eyes. Finally he said, "I'm going to have to put him down."

"Just because he's cross-eyed?" exclaimed the owner.

"No," said the vet. "Because he's really, really heavy."

Druggist: Sir, excuse me for asking, but I've noticed lately that you come to my drugstore every week and buy two dozen condoms.

Customer: Yes?

Druggist: I know it's none of my business, but how can you possibly use that many condoms in a week?

Customer: I feed them to my poodle, and now when she poops, she poops in little plastic bags.

The dog owner called his veterinarian in a panic. "Doctor! Help! My dog just ate the TV remote!"

"Don't worry, I'll be right over," replied the DVM.

"Wait!" said the dog owner. "What do I do in the meantime?"

Said the vet, "Read a magazine."

Mr. Jones asked, "Got anything to cure fleas on a dog?"

"That depends," said the slow-minded vet. "What's wrong with them?"

A man asked the vet to remove his dog's tail. The vet inquired why.

"My mother-in-law is visiting in a few weeks," replied the man, "and I want to eliminate any possible indication that she is welcome."

Miss Primm, a single woman of advanced years, had as her closest companion a pretty French poodle named Gigi. For a number of weeks, the dog had seemed out of sorts, and the concerned Miss Primm took her to the veterinarian.

"Tell me, doctor," she implored. "What is wrong with my Gigi?"

The DVM found himself a bit abashed with regards to the elderly woman's spinsterhood.

"Well, Miss Primm," he fumbled, "there is a time in the life of a bi—, of a lady dog, when companionship is called for. Gigi should be introduced to a gentleman dog."

"I'm not sure I could accommodate two dogs in my house," said Miss Primm, blushing.

"Don't worry, Miss Primm, there are places where such arrangements may be made, and with boy dogs of the best breeding."

"Well, all right, doctor, but will I need to be there?"

"Not at all. The dogs know exactly what to do," said the vet. "But there is one thing I must warn you about—the stud fees can be high."

With a look of outraged disbelief, Miss Primm rose to her feet and said, "You mean *Gigi* pays?"

Sign in a Veterinarian's waiting room:
"Be back in 5 minutes. Sit! Stay!"

A piece of grass a day keeps
the vet away.

—UNKNOWN DOG

YOUR PET'S PET PEEVES

- Blaming the flatulence on me. Not funny.

- Tricks involving balancing food on my nose. Stop it.

- Getting mad when I sniff your guests' crotches. Sorry, I haven't mastered the handshake thing yet.

- Picking up the piles in the yard. Do you know how far behind schedule that puts me?

- The fake-out tennis ball throw. Wow, you fooled a dog!

- Doggie sweaters. Like you haven't noticed the fur.

- Doggie haircuts involving ribbons. Now you know why we chew your stuff when you're not home.

- Running away during a perfectly good leg humping.

- Invisible fences. Why must you screw with us?

- Acting disgusted when I lick myself. We both know you're just jealous.

dogma

JOKES ABOUT DOGS AND RELIGION

It was a slow day in Heaven, so God phoned Satan to see what was going on down there.

"It's slow here, too," said Satan.

"Well," God said, "I think a dog show might be fun."

"Sounds good," says Satan, "but why are you calling me? You've got all the dogs up there." "I know," answered God. "But you've got all the judges."

Late one night, a burglar broke into a house he thought was empty. The thief tiptoed through the living room, but froze in his tracks when he heard a voice call out, "Jesus is watching you."

Then silence returned to the house, and, after waiting several minutes, the burglar crept forward once more. "Jesus is watching you," the voice called again.

Paralyzed with fear, the burglar stopped dead again, and looked all around. In a dark corner, he spotted a bird cage. In the cage was a parrot. He asked the parrot, "Was that you who said Jesus is watching me?"

"Yes," said the parrot. The burglar breathed a

sigh of relief, then asked the parrot, "What's your name?" "Dwayne," said the bird. "That's a dumb name for a parrot," sneered the burglar. "What idiot named you Dwayne?"

The parrot said, "The same idiot who named the rottweiler Jesus."

A fundamentalist Christian couple felt it was important to own an equally fundamental pet. So they went shopping, and, at a kennel specializing in that particular type of canine, they found a dog they liked quite a lot. When they commanded the animal to fetch the Bible, he complied in a flash. When they asked him to look up Psalm 23, he responded equally quickly, using his paws deftly. Impressed, the couple purchased the dog and went home.

That night they had friends over. The couple was so proud of their new fundamentalist pet, they called the dog in and showed him off a bit.

Their friends were also impressed, and asked

whether the dog could do any of the usual dog tricks as well. This stopped the couple cold, as they hadn't thought about "normal" tricks. "Well," said the husband, "let's see." Once more the couple called the dog, then pronounced the command, "Heel!" Quick as a wink, the dog jumped up, put his paw on the man's forehead, closed his eyes in concentration, and bowed his head.

A clergyman was walking down the street when he came upon a group of boys surrounding a dog.

"What are you boys doing with that dog?" the clergyman demanded.

"This dog is a neighbor-hood stray," said one of the boys. "We all want him for a pet, but only one of us can take him home. So we decided that which-ever one of us can tell the biggest lie will get to keep the dog."

The reverend was appalled. "You boys shouldn't be having a lying contest!" he exclaimed, and commenced a lengthy sermon about the sin of lying that ended with the statement, "When I was your age, I never told a lie."

There was dead silence.

Just as the clergyman was beginning to think

he'd gotten through to the youngsters, the smallest boy sighed deeply and said, "All right, give him the dog."

Patrick was the most absent-minded altar boy Father O'Hara had ever seen. But he meant well, and the priest was keen on giving him the chance to prove himself. "At mass tomorrow," the priest instructed, "when I sing 'And God's angels lit the candles,' you light the candles in the back of the church. Understood?"

Patrick nodded his head, and he and Father prayed for his success.

The next day, after the congregants were settled in their pews, Father O'Hara began the mass. Finally, it was Patrick's moment. The priest sang out, "And God's angels lit the candles!"

Nothing happened. The priest said it again: "And God's angels lit the candles!" Still the candles remained unlit. Annoyed, Father bellowed it out one more time: "And God's angels lit the candles!"

Then, from behind the last pew, Patrick's small voice carried across the church: "And your dog pissed on the matches!"

A man and his dog were walking down a road enjoying the scenery when it suddenly occurred to the man that he was dead. He remembered dying, and also recalled that his dog had been dead for years. He wondered where the road led.

After a long walk, they came to a white marble wall along one side of the road, with a magnificent gate that looked like it was made of mother of pearl. The street beyond the gate looked as if it was made of gold. The man and dog continued walking. As they got closer, they saw a man at a desk beside the gate. The first man called out, "Excuse me, where are we?"

"This is heaven, sir," was the reply.

"Wow!" the traveler exclaimed. "Um, would you happen to have some water?"

"Of course, sir. Come in. I'll have some ice

water brought right up." The man began to open the gate.

"Can my friend come in, too?" the traveler asked, gesturing toward his dog.

"I'm sorry, sir. We don't accept pets."

The man thought a moment, and then turned back toward the road with his dog. They continued the way they'd been going. After another long walk, they came to a farm with an old wooden gate that was wide open. As they approached the gate, they saw a man inside, sitting against a tree reading a book.

"Excuse me!" said the traveler. "Do you have any water?"

"Sure, there's a pump over there." The reader pointed to a place that couldn't be seen from outside the gate. "Come on in."

"How about my friend here?" The traveler gestured to his dog.

"There should be a bowl by the pump."

They went through the gate, and sure enough, there was an old-fashioned hand pump with a bowl beside it. The traveler filled the bowl, let his dog drink, then had some water himself. When they were done, he and the dog walked back to the man by the tree.

"What do you call this place?" the traveler asked.

"This is heaven," was the answer.

"Well, that's funny," the traveler said. "The man down the road said that was heaven, too."

"Oh, you mean the place with the pearly gate? Nope. That's hell."

"Doesn't it make you mad that they use the same name?"

"No. I can see how some might think so, but we're just happy that they screen out the folks who'd leave their best friends behind."

And Adam said, "Lord, when I was in the garden, you walked with me every day. Now I do not see you anymore. I am lonesome here, and it is difficult for me to remember how much you love me."

And God said, "No problem! I will create a companion for you that will be with you forever and that will be a reflection of my love for you, so you will know I love you, even when you cannot see me. Regardless of how selfish, childish, and unlovable you may be, this new companion will accept you as you are and will love you as I do, in spite of yourself."

And God created a new animal to be a

companion for Adam. And the new animal was pleased to be with Adam and wagged its tail. And Adam said, "But Lord, I have already named all the animals in the Kingdom. All the good names are taken and I cannot think of a name for this new animal."

And God said, "No problem! Because I have created this new animal to be a reflection of my love for you, his name will be a reflection of my own name, and you will call him DOG."

And DOG lived with Adam and was a companion to him and loved him. And Adam was comforted. And God was pleased. And DOG wagged his tail.

After a while, it came to pass that Adam's guardian angel came to the Lord and said, "Lord, Adam has become filled with pride. He struts like a peacock and believes he is worthy of adoration. DOG has indeed taught him that he is loved, but no one has taught him humility."

And the Lord said, "No problem! I will create for him a companion that will be with him forever and will see him as he is. The companion will remind him of his limitations, so he will know that he is not worthy of adoration."

And God created CAT. And CAT would not obey Adam. And when Adam gazed into CAT's eyes, he was reminded that he was not a supreme being. And Adam learned humility.

And God was pleased. And Adam was greatly improved. And DOG was content. And CAT did not care one way or the other.

Q: What do you get when you cross an insomniac, an agnostic, and a dyslexic?

A: Someone who stays up all night wondering if there is a Dog.

—GROUCHO MARX

PRAYER OF THE DOG
Canine Letters to God

- Dear God, when we get to Heaven, can we sit on your sofa? Or is it the same old story?

- Dear God, are there mailmen in Heaven? If so, will I have to apologize?

- Dear God, is it true that in Heaven, dining room tables have on-ramps?

- Dear God, are there dogs on other planets, or are we alone? I've howled at the moon and stars for years, but all I ever hear back is the yappy dog across the street.

- Dear God, more meatballs, less spaghetti, please.

more dog riddles

Q: Where do you find a dog with no legs?

A: The same place you lost him.

Q: What do you call a dog with no legs?

A: Don't matter. He ain't going to come anyway.

Q: What can you do with a dog with no legs?

A: Take it for a drag.

Q: What do you call a dog with no hind legs and balls of steel?

A: Sparky.

Q: Where do dogs buy their underwear?

A: K-9 Mart.

Q: What do you get when you cross dogs with fountain pens?

A: Ink Spots.

Q: What do you get when you cross a dog with an omelet?

A: Pooched eggs.

Q: What do you get when you cross a dog with a sprinter?

A: The 100-yard dachshund.

Top 10 Names for Male Dogs

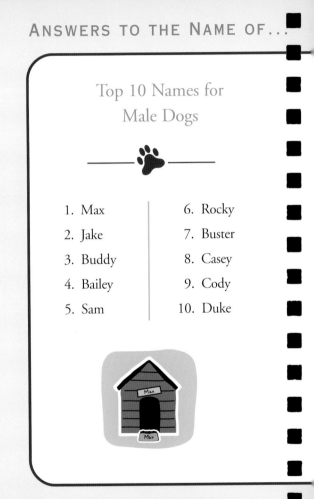

1. Max
2. Jake
3. Buddy
4. Bailey
5. Sam

6. Rocky
7. Buster
8. Casey
9. Cody
10. Duke

Top 10 Names for Female Dogs

1. Maggie	6. Daisy
2. Molly	7. Ginger
3. Lady	8. Abby
4. Sadie	9. Sasha
5. Lucy	10. Sandy

Fun Names for Dogs

Boris

Calamity

Clouseau

Dammit
(so you can yell "Dammit, get in here")

Diablo

Diva

Furrgus

McGoo

Miss Chievous

Mr. Darcy

Mr. Hyde

Nemo

P. D.
(Puppy Dog)

Radar

Watson

Names for Big Dogs

Attila	Lurch
Fang	Shamu
Hummer	Tank
Jabba	Texas
Kong	Worf

Names for Small Dogs

Boo-Boo	Napoleon
Conan	Pipsqueak
Fang	Proton
Gizmo	Shorty
Laptop	Twinkie

Names for Pairs of Dogs

Ben & Jerry

Bogie & Bacall

Bonnie & Clyde

Butch & Sundance

Dow & Jones

Hunky & Dory

Johnson & Boswell

Pete & Repeat

Posh & Becks

Rock & Roll

Smith & Wesson

THAT DOG DON'T HUNT
Things Dogs Don't Understand

- It's wrong to back Auntie into the corner and guard her.

- The cat has a right to be in the living room.

- It's wrong to play tug-of-war with Dad's underwear when he's on the toilet.

- The garbage man is not stealing our stuff.

- We do not have a doorbell. It's wrong to bark every time we hear one on TV.

- It's wrong to bite the policeman's hand when he reaches in for Mom's license and registration.

dogs at work

A preschool teacher was driving a minivan of kids one day when a fire truck zoomed past. Sitting in the front seat of the fire truck was a Dalmatian. The children began discussing what the dog's duties might be.

"They use him to keep crowds back," said one youngster.

"No," said another, "he's for good luck."

"No, silly," concluded a third, "they use the dog to find the fire hydrant!"

Just finishing his shift, the policeman parked his van in front of the station. As the officer gathered his gear, his K-9 partner began to bark. The officer saw a little boy staring in at the cop and his German shepherd.

"Is that a dog in there?" the boy asked.

"That's right," the officer replied.

Puzzled, the boy looked at the policeman, then at the dog.

Finally he asked, "What'd he do?"

Returning home from work, a blonde was shocked to find her house ransacked and burglarized. She called 911 at once to report the crime. The dispatcher broadcast the call, and a K-9 unit patrolling nearby was first on the scene.

As the K-9 officer approached the house with his German shepherd, the blonde opened the door, clapped a hand to her head, and moaned, "I come home from work to find all my possessions stolen, I call for help, and what do they do? They send a BLIND policeman!"

A blind fellow walking down a Toronto street commanded his guide dog to turn right into what he thought was the subway entrance. But he'd somehow gotten the directions wrong and found himself and the dog in a dead-end alley. A passerby happened along and asked if he could assist.

"Yes, thanks," said the blind man. "I was trying to get to the subway."

The man leaned over the dog and said slowly and distinctly in the canine's ear, "Take . . . him . . . to . . . the . . . subway."

As told to an unknown guide dog trainer

Q: What do you call a German shepherd in jeans and a sweater?

A: A plainclothes police dog.

what the wags say

QUIPS AND QUOTES ABOUT DOGS

My dog is half pit bull, half poodle. Not much of a watchdog, but a vicious gossip!

—CRAIG SHOEMAKER

I hope if dogs ever take over the world, and they chose a king, they don't just go by size, because I bet there are some Chihuahuas with some good ideas.

—JACK HANDEY, *DEEP THOUGHTS*

Never trust a dog to watch your food.

—PATRICK, AGE 10

Always drink upstream from the pack.

—AUTHOR UNKNOWN

Never stand between a dog
and the hydrant.

—JOHN PEERS

If you want the best seat in the
house, move the dog.

—AUTHOR UNKNOWN

Dogs are the leaders of the planet.
If you see two life forms,
one of them's making a poop, the
other's carrying it for him, who
would you assume is in charge?

—JERRY SEINFELD

In dog years, I'm dead.

—AUTHOR UNKNOWN

Dachshund: A half-a-dog high
and a dog-and-a-half long.

—H. L. MENCKEN

No one appreciates the very special genius of your conversation as the dog does.

—CHRISTOPHER MORLEY

There is no snooze button on a dog who wants breakfast.

—AUTHOR UNKNOWN

When a dog wags her tail and barks at the same time, how do you know which end to believe?

—AUTHOR UNKNOWN

When it's raining cats and dogs, be sure not to step in the poodles.

—AUTHOR UNKNOWN

If you get to thinking you're a person of some influence, try ordering somebody else's dog around.

—WILL ROGERS

To a dog, the whole world is a smell.

—AUTHOR UNKNOWN

In order to really enjoy a dog, one doesn't merely try to train him to be semi-human. The point of it is to open oneself to the possibility of becoming partly a dog.

—EDWARD HOAGLAND

The other day I saw two dogs walk over to a parking meter. One says to the other, "How do you like that? Pay toilets!"

—DAVE STARR

They say the dog is man's best friend. I don't believe that. How many of your friends have you neutered?

—LARRY REEB

Mrs. Campbell once attempted to smuggle her pet Pekingese through customs by tucking him inside the upper part of her cape. "Everything was going splendidly," she later remarked, "until my bosom barked."

—BEATRICE STELLA CAMPBELL

Never moon a werewolf.

—MIKE BINDER

puppy love

JOKES ABOUT DOGS AND ROMANCE

For months he'd admired his love from afar. Now, at last, he'd gathered the courage to ask her the question.

"There are advantages to being a bachelor," he began, "but there comes a time when one longs for the companionship of another— one who will regard one as perfect, as an idol. One to be treated as absolute property; one who'll be faithful when times are hard, and who will share one's joys and sorrows."

Much to his delight, he saw an encouraging gleam in her eye. She nodded enthusiastically.

"So you're thinking of buying a dog?" she said. "A fabulous idea—do let me help you choose one!"

A young man was nervous about being invited to dinner to meet his girlfriend's parents. In fact, he was so worried, he couldn't help passing wind throughout the meal.

The first time he did it, his girlfriend's father turned to the family dog sitting next to the table and said, "Rover, move away."

The boyfriend was most grateful to the father for getting him out of the awkward situation.

But a minute or so later, the boy dropped another one. Again, the father turned to the dog, and said, "Rover, move away, will you." Again, the young man was grateful.

A couple of minutes later, the young suitor let out a real snorter—louder and smellier than the two before. The father turned to the dog and said, "For crying out loud, Rover. You'd better hurry up and move away before he craps all over you!"

The most affectionate creature
in the world is a wet dog.

—AMBROSE BIERCE

Three alpha males are swaggering down the street when they see a gorgeous French poodle.

Each of the males dashes to be the first to reach her, but all three end up in front of her at the same time, slobbering all over themselves.

Aware of her effect on the threesome, the poodle tells them, "Whichever one of you can use the words 'liver' and 'cheese' in an imaginative, intelligent sentence can go out with me."

The first, a muscular Doberman, says, "*Ich liebe* liver *und* cheese."

"Oh, how childish," said the Poodle. "That shows no intelligence whatsoever."

She turns to the second, a distinguished-looking English bulldog, and says, "What about you?"

"Truthfully, madam, I despise liver and cheese," states the bulldog.

"My, my," says the poodle. "This is hopeless." She then turns to the third dog and says, "How about *you*, cutie?"

The last of the three, a Chihuahua, gives her a wink, turns to the Doberman and the bulldog, and says, "Liver alone. Cheese mine."

Just give me a comfortable couch,
a dog, a good book, and a woman.
Then if you can get the dog to go
somewhere and read the book,
I might have a little fun!

—GROUCHO MARX

IN THE DOGHOUSE

Why Dogs Are Better than Men

- Dogs think you are a culinary genius.

- Dogs understand if some of their friends cannot come inside.

- Dogs are happy with any movie you rent, because they know the most important thing is that you're together.

- Dogs do not have problems expressing affection in public.

- Dogs don't brag about whom they have slept with.

- Dogs don't play games with you except fetch (and they never laugh at how you throw).

- Dogs don't mind if you do the driving (and they never step on the imaginary brake).

- Gorgeous dogs don't know they're gorgeous.

- Dogs mean it when they kiss you.

- You are never suspicious of your dog's dreams.

BONES OF CONTENTION

Why Dogs Are Better than Women

- Dogs don't mind if you use their shampoo.

- Dogs like it when you leave lots of things on the floor.

- Dogs love it when your friends come over.

- Dogs think you sing great.

- A dog's time in the bathroom is confined to a quick drink.

- Dogs don't worry about germs.

- Dogs understand that using your instincts is better than asking for directions.

- Dogs like to snoop outside, instead of in your wallet, desk, and the backs of your dresser drawers.

- Dogs never need to examine the relationship.

- Dogs don't let magazine articles guide their lives.

- Dogs don't shop.

tall tails

A group of geezers were discussing dogs, and the tales were getting pretty "tall" when one of the oldsters took the lead.

"Smith," he said, "had a most intelligent dog. One night Smith's house caught fire. All was chaos. Smith and his wife ran for the children and got them out in quick order. Everyone was safe, but Smith's old dog Rover dashed back into the flames. Soon the animal reappeared, scorched, burned, and with—what do you think?"

"We give up," cried the eager audience.

"With the fire insurance policy wrapped in a damp towel, gentlemen."

"Horses!" said the Yankee to the Canadian. "Guess you can't talk to me about horses. I once had a mare that could beat the express train."

"That's nothing!" said the Canuck. "I was out twenty miles from my house on my farm one day when a frightful storm came up. I turned my pony's head for home, and do you know, he raced the storm so close for the last five miles I didn't feel a drop, while my dog, just ten yards behind, had to swim the whole distance."

A man in New York was grumbling about the heat. Said another who had just returned from a trip down South:

"Hot! Boy, you don't know what hot is. One day last week in Mississippi, I saw a dog chasing a cat and they were both walking."

It's so dry the trees are bribing the dogs.

—SOUTHERN EXPRESSION

A DOG'S DIARY

DAY 1

8AM—All right! Breakfast! My favorite thing!

10AM—All right! Walk with Mom! My favorite thing!

12NOON—All right! A car ride! My favorite thing!

2PM—All right! The kids! My favorite thing!

4PM—All right! Dad's home! My favorite thing!

6PM—All right! Dinner! My favorite thing!

8PM—All right! Sleepy time! My favorite thing!

DAY 2

8AM—All right! Breakfast! My favorite thing!

10AM—All right! Walk with Mom! My favorite thing!

12NOON—All right! A car ride! My favorite thing!

2PM—All right! The kids! My favorite thing!

4PM— All right! Dad's home! My favorite thing!

6PM—All right! Dinner! My favorite thing!

8PM—All right! Sleepy time! My favorite thing!

DAY 3

8AM—All right! Breakfast! My favorite thing!

10AM—All right! Walk with Mom! My favorite thing!

12NOON—All right! A car ride! My favorite thing!

2PM—All right! The kids! My favorite thing!

4PM—All right! Dad's home! My favorite thing!

6PM—All right! Dinner! My favorite thing!

8PM— All right! Sleepy time! My favorite thing!

DAY 4

8AM—All right! Breakfast! My favorite thing!

10AM—All right! Walk with Mom! My favorite thing!

12NOON—All right! A car ride! My favorite thing!

2PM—All right! The kids! My favorite thing!

4PM—All right! Dad's home! My favorite thing!

6PM—All right! Dinner! My favorite thing!

8PM—All right! Sleepy time! My favorite thing!

pup-pourri

Puppies

Customer: "Has this dog a good pedigree?"

Shop Owner: "Has he? Say, if that dog could talk, he wouldn't speak to either of us."

Sign in pet store:

"Buy one dog, get one flea."

"Sorry, old man, my hen got loose and scratched up your garden."
"That's all right, my dog ate your hen."
"Fine! I just ran over your dog and killed him."

"Lay, down, pup. Lay down. That's a good doggie. Lay down, I tell you."

"Mister, you'll have to say 'Lie down.' He's a Boston terrier."

Uncle: "Does your puppy have a pedigree?"

Nephew: "Sure."

Uncle: "Do you have papers for it?"

Nephew: "All over the house."

First neighbor: "Did you say your dog's bark was worse than his bite?"

Second neighbor: "Yes."

First neighbor: "Then for Heaven's sake, don't let him bark. He just bit me."

Caught in an avalanche, two skiers are about to panic when they spot a St. Bernard lumbering toward them through the snow, a keg of brandy at its neck.

"Look!" says one. "Man's best friend!"

"Yes!" says the second. "And it's being carried by a dog!"

Customer: "I ran an advertisement for my lost dog in your newspaper here. Has anything been heard of it? I offered a reward of $100."

Clerk: "Sorry, ma'am, all the editors and reporters are out looking for the dog."

Economics professor: "Give me an example of indirect taxation."

Freshman: "The dog tax, sir."

Prof: "How is that?"

Frosh: "The dog does not have to pay it."

"Boy," said the traveling stranger to a disobedient young hillbilly, "didn't you hear your father speak to you?"

"Oh, y-a-a-s," drawled the youth, "but Ah don't mind nothing he says. Ma don't neither, an' twixt both of us we've just about got the dawg so he don't."

Up in Maine a journalist came across a lonely cabin and interviewed its inhabitant with a view to writing up the locality.

"Whose house is this?" he asked.

"Moggs."

"What is it built of?"

"Logs."

Any animals natural to the locality?"

"Frogs."

"What sort of soil have you?"

"Bogs."

"How about the climate?"

"Fogs."

"What do you live on chiefly?"

"Hogs."

"Have you any friends?"

"Dogs."

Dumb dog.

I bought a dog whistle. He won't use it.

A dad goes into a pet store and asks if he can return the puppy he got for his son. The owner replies, "I'm sorry, sir, but we've already sold your son to someone else."

It was the end of the school year, and the kindergarten teacher was receiving gifts from her young pupils. First, the florist's son handed her a beautifully wrapped package. The teacher held out the gift, shook it, and said, "I think it's flowers. Am I right?"

"Yes," said the boy.

Her second gift was from the daughter of a sweet shop owner. The teacher held the ribbon-bedecked box aloft, shook it, and said, "I think it's sweets. Am I right?"

"Yes," said the girl.

The third gift was from the son of a local liquor store owner. Once again, it was beautifully done up with ribbons and bows. The teacher held it above her head, and shook it, but as she did so, it began to

leak. She touched a drop with her finger and put it on her tongue. "I think it's wine. Am I right?"

"No, Teacher," said the boy.

So the teacher tasted another drop of the leakage. "Is it Champagne?"

"No, Teacher," said the boy.

The teacher tasted another drop, but, unable to recognize it, admitted defeat. "I give up. What is it?"

The boy said, "It's a puppy."

Two dogs were walking down the street when one suddenly crossed the road, sniffed a lamp post for a minute, then crossed back again.

"What was that all about?" asked the other dog.

"Just checking my messages."

A stranger entering a little country store noticed a sign on the door that said, "Danger! Beware of Dog!" Inside, he saw a harmless old hound dog sleeping on the floor near the cash register.

The stranger asked the storekeeper, "Is that the dog customers are supposed to beware of?"

"Yes, that's him," was the reply.

"That does not look like a dangerous dog to

me," said the bemused stranger. "Why in the world would you post that sign?" "Because," said the owner, "before I posted that sign, people kept tripping over him."

Researchers have discovered that dogs can comprehend a vocabulary of 2,000 words, whereas cats can only comprehend 25 to 50 words. No one has asked how many words the researchers can comprehend.

A man wrote a letter to a small hotel in a New England town, which he planned to visit during his vacation. He wrote, "I would very much like to bring my dog with me. He is well groomed and well behaved. Would you be willing to permit me to keep him in my room with me at night?"

An immediate reply came from the hotel owner, who said, "I've been operating this hotel for many years. In all that time, I've never had a dog steal towels, bedclothes, silverware, or pictures off the walls. I've never had to evict a dog in the middle of the night for being drunk and disorderly. And I've never had a dog run out on a hotel bill. Yes, your dog is welcome at my hotel, and if your dog will vouch for you, you're welcome to stay here, too!"

A young woman was visiting a blonde friend who'd recently acquired two dogs, and asked what their names were.

The blonde informed her that one dog was

named Rolex and the other was named Timex.

"Whoever heard of someone naming dogs like that?" her friend commented.

"Halloo!" retorted the blonde. "They're watch dogs!"

An attorney's dog, running off its leash, dashed into a butcher shop and stole a roast right off the counter.

The butcher goes to the attorney's office and asks, "If a dog steals meat from my store, do I have a right to demand payment from its owner?"

"Absolutely," said the lawyer.

"Then you owe me ten dollars. Your dog stole a roast from me today."

Without a word, the attorney paid him.

A week later, the butcher received a letter from the lawyer. Opening it, he read, "Invoice: Dog Law Consultation: $100."

A man comes home from work one day to find his dog with the neighbor's pet rabbit, dead, in its mouth. The man panics, thinking the neighbor is going to hate him forever, so he takes the filthy, mangled rabbit into the house, gives it a bath, and blow dries its fur. He sneaks the rabbit back into its cage at the neighbor's house, and hopes they'll think it died of natural causes.

The next weekend, the neighbor is outside and asks the man, "Did you hear that Fluffy died?"

The man hesitates, then says, "Um, no. What happened?"

"We found him dead in his cage last week," the neighbor says. "But the weird thing is that the day after we buried him, someone dug him up, gave him a bath, and put him back in the cage. There must be some really sick people out there!"

A man comes into a tavern and puts his legless dog down on the bar. The bartender comes over to take his order and asks, "What's your dog's name?"

"He doesn't have one," says the man.

The bartender fixes a second round and asks again, "Come on. What's the dog's name?"

"I told you, he doesn't have one," says the man.

Over the third round, the barkeep leans over the bar and comments, "I just find it hard to believe. Every dog has a name."

"Not this dog," says the man. "What's the use of it? He can't come when I call."

First Mailman: "A dog bit me on the leg this morning!"

Second Mailman: "Did you put anything on it?"

First Mailman: "No, he liked it plain!"

"If a dog is happy," said the teacher, "it wags its tail. What does a goose do?"

Blurted little Michael, "Piss the dog off?"

A woman was walking down the street when she noticed an unusual funeral procession approaching a nearby cemetery. A black hearse was followed by a second hearse; behind the two vehicles was a woman walking a mastiff on a leash. Behind the woman and dog were dozens of other women, walking single file. Beside herself with curiosity, the first woman respectfully approached the lady with the dog and said, "I'm sorry for your loss! I hate to disturb you at this time, but I must say I've never seen a funeral like this. Whose funeral is it?"

The woman replied, "That first hearse is for my husband."

"What happened to him?"

The woman replied, "My dog attacked and killed him."

The first woman inquired further. "Who is in the second hearse?"

The woman answered, "My mother-in-law. She was trying to help my husband, and the dog turned on her."

There was a moment of silence. The first woman spoke again.

"May I borrow that dog?"

"Get in line."

An elderly woman is sitting in her rocking chair on the front porch, reflecting on her many years, when out of the blue, a fairy godmother appears before her and tells her she can have any three wishes she wants.

"My stars!" says the little old lady. "Well, I guess I'd like to be rich."

And poof! Her rocking chair turns into gold.

"And I guess I wouldn't mind being changed into a lovely young princess."

Poof! The old lady became a beautiful young damsel.

"You have a third wish," the fairy godmother says, just as the woman's faithful old dog crosses the porch in front of them.

"Can you turn my dog into a handsome prince?" asks the woman.

Poof! Sure enough! There before her stands a veritable Adonis, handsomer than her wildest dreams.

With a dazzling smile that makes her knees weak, the young prince saunters across the porch and whispers in her ear, "Aren't you sorry you had me neutered?"

One evening a knight, riding to the rescue of a damsel in distress, ran into a violent storm. Thunder boomed. The rain poured down. Without warning, a bolt of lightning hit the knight's horse. It collapsed and died.

With his saddle slung over his shoulder, the knight slogged his way to the nearest village and pounded on the door of the inn. The landlord answered, and the dripping knight staggered inside.

"Landlord!" he gasped. "Give me your finest horse, no matter the cost!"

"Sorry, sire, we're right out of horses!" "Then give me a mule, or a donkey!" "Sorry, sire, no mules or donkeys neither. Not even a pony!"

"Then what have you got?" begged the knight.

"Just a giant Irish wolfhound, sire. Here he is,

by the fire. Good boy, Thor!" the landlord said.

The dog rose to its feet. It was huge, as big as a pony—big enough to carry the knight. But it looked as if it had tangled with one too many wolves in its day—it limped along on three legs. And it, too, had been out in the rain. Its coat absolutely reeked; the smell of wet dog fur nearly made the knight throw up. And the panting beast's breath was so foul it nearly made him faint. Still, chivalry called. The damsel awaited. Gamely, the knight strapped the saddle on the hound and threw his leg over the animal's back. The dog swayed towards the entrance. The landlord opened the door, peered out into the torrents of rain, and looked back at the hound. Suddenly, he slammed the door shut again, and shook his head.

"Sorry, sire, I just can't do it!" he said.

"Can't do what?"

"I just can't let a knight go out on a dog like this!"

Two nuns from overseas have just arrived in the USA by boat. One says to the other, "I hear that the people of this country actually eat dogs." "Good heavens!" her companion replies, "but, if we are to live in America, we may as well do as the Americans do."

Nodding, the mother superior leads the way to a nearby hot dog cart. "Two, please," she says.

The vendor, only too pleased to oblige, wraps both franks in foil, and hands them to the nuns. The sisters find a bench, sit, and begin to unwrap their "dogs." The mother superior stares at hers for a moment, blushes, nudges the other nun, and whispers, "What part did you get?"

I saw a woman and a dog and asked her, "Does your dog bite?"

"No," she replied.

I petted the dog, and he bit me.

Furious, I exclaimed, "Hey! Didn't you say your dog doesn't bite?"

She said, "He's not my dog."

One dry, dusty day in the Old West, a dog walked into a saloon and said, "Gimme a beer."

"We don't serve dogs here, you mongrel," snapped the bartender.

The dog dropped a silver dollar on the bar and said, "I got money. I want a beer."
"I said, we don't serve dogs here. Vamoose."
The dog growled. Suddenly, the cowpoke on

the next barstool pulled out a gun and shot the dog in the foot. The dog yelped and made for the exit.

The next day, the saloon doors swung open. In strode the dog, with a bandaged paw, wearing a black cowboy hat, black cowboy boots, and a six-shooter.

"What do *you* want?" asked the bartender.

Cocking the pistol, the dog snarled, "I'm lookin' fer the man who shot my paw."

GOING TO THE DOGS
Newspaper Misprints?

FREE PUPPIES: Part German Shepherd, part Alaskan Hussy.

FREE PUPPIES: 1/2 cocker spaniel, 1/2 sneaky neighbor dog.

FREE YORKSHIRE TERRIER: 6 years old. Unpleasant little dog. Bites.

GERMAN SHEPHERD: 85 pounds, neutered, speaks German, free.

FOUND: Dirty white dog, looks like a rat, been out awhile, better be a reward.

DOGGEREL

May be sung to the tune of
"My Favorite Things"

Biscuits in boxes, and pig ears, and tuna,

Bird seed, and pasta,
and PB by the spoon-a,

Used paper plates that once
held chicken wings,

These are a few of my favorite things.

Tennis balls, Frisbees, and leftover toast,

Litter box crunchies and
purloined pot roast

Socks from the hamper and strange
stuff that clings,

These are a few of my favorite things.

Watching for mailmen, squirrels,
and the cat,

Patrolling my turf is just where it's at

Barking at neighbors and
birds on the wing,

These are a few of my favorite things.

CHORUS

When it thunders,
And I'm under
the bed when the folks are away,
I simply remember my favorite things
and then I will not stray.

THE SHAGGY DOG

While reading an advertisement in the local newspaper for a large, shaggy lost dog, a hobo noticed that there was a shaggy dog of similar proportions smelling his shoes. Since the ad offered a substantial reward, the hobo grabbed the dog by its collar and proceeded at once to the address given in the ad.

When he reached the address, he knocked at the door. A butler answered. The hobo said, "Here is the lost dog you advertised for."

"Not at all," the butler replied, nose in the air. "When we said shaggy, we didn't mean *that* shaggy."